Anatomy of a SHIPWRECK

by Sean McCollum

Consultant:
John D. Broadwater
Maritime Archaeologist
Spritsail Consulting
Williamsburg, Virginia

CAPSTONE PRESS
a capstone imprint

Velocity is published by Capstone Press,
151 Good Counsel Drive, P.O. Box 669, Mankato, Minnesota 56002.
www.capstonepub.com

032010
005741WZF10

Books published by Capstone Press are manufactured with paper
containing at least 10 percent post-consumer waste.

Library of Congress Cataloging-in-Publication Data
McCollum, Sean.
   Anatomy of a shipwreck / by Sean McCollum.
      p. cm.—(Velocity. disasters.)
   Includes bibliographical references and index.
   Summary: "Describes the science behind shipwrecks, including causes, prevention, and
famous shipwrecks"—Provided by publisher.
   ISBN 978-1-4296-4794-6 (library binding)
   1. Shipwrecks—Juvenile literature. I. Title. II. Series.
   G525.M24 2011
   363.12'3—dc22   2010003393

Editorial Credits
Mandy Robbins, editor; Heidi Thompson, designer; Svetlana Zhurkin, media researcher;
   Eric Manske, production specialist

Photo Credits
Alamy/Ron Buskirk, 26; AP Photo, 5, 42–43; AP Photo/Jim Paulin, 32–33; BigStockPhoto/
Rafael Ramirez Lee, 39 (top); Capstone Press, 15 (middle), 16, 19, 21, 29, 33 (inset),
34–35; Corbis/epa/Akhtar Soomro, cover (bottom); Dreamstime/Durdenimages, 12; Getty
Images/General Photographic Agency, 38; Getty Images/Time Life Pictures/Loomis Dean,
40; Getty Images/Time Life Pictures/Yale Joel, 41; iStockphoto/k-pics, 24 (inset); Library
of Congress, 9, 17; Newscom, 8, 18 (bottom); Newscom/AFP/STR, 44; Newscom/AFP/
USCG, 36; Newscom/Digital Press/Ramon Villero, 37; Newscom/Getty Images/AFP/HO,
45; Newscom/KRT, 10, 11 (bottom); Newscom/KRT/Courtesy of RMS Titanic, Inc., 4;
Newscom/UPI Photo/USCG/Petty Officer 3rd Class Gail Sinner, 20; Newscom/Zuma/
San Diego Union-Tribune/Howard Lipin, 27; NOAA, cover (top), 6–7; Shutterstock/
Armin Lehnhoff, 24–25; Shutterstock/criben, 22–23; Shutterstock/Darryl Brooks, 18 (top);
Shutterstock/Igor Chaikovskiy, 14–15; Shutterstock/Jon Milnes, 39 (bottom); Shutterstock/
Khoroshunova Olga (ocean), 34–35; Shutterstock/Nikonov (metal background),
throughout; Shutterstock/Oculo (mosaic design element), cover and throughout;
Shutterstock/Oleksandr Kalinichenko, 28; Shutterstock/Sebastian Kaulitzki (scratched metal
background), back cover and throughout; Shutterstock/sf2301420max, 13; Shutterstock/
Stanislav E. Petrov (cement background), throughout; Shutterstock/Steve Estvanik, 30–31;
Shutterstock/Terence Mendoza, 11 (top)

TABLE OF CONTENTS

Introduction: Fascinated by Shipwrecks   4

Chapter 1: The Sinking of the *Titanic*   6

Chapter 2: Why Ships Sink   12

Chapter 3: Building a Safer Ship   22

Chapter 4: On the Bridge   28

Chapter 5: Rescue at Sea   32

Chapter 6: Famous Shipwrecks   38

Glossary   46
Read More   47
Internet Sites   47
Index   48

FASCINATED BY SHIPWRECKS

On August 10, 1998, a piece of history slowly rose from the ocean floor. It had been 86 years since the great ship sank in the Atlantic Ocean. Large bags had been inflated with a special liquid to float a wall of rusted steel upward. Finally, the 20-ton (18-metric ton) section of *Titanic*'s hull saw daylight once more. It was about 25 feet (7.6 meters) long and 13 feet (4 m) high. Three of the portholes still had some glass in them.

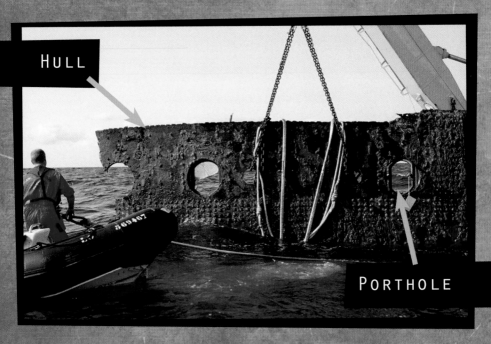

HULL

PORTHOLE

Today this big piece of *Titanic*'s hull travels to museums. It is part of an exhibit of artifacts retrieved from the wreck. Crowds of people come to view these objects.

Shipwrecks have always fascinated people. Stories of bravery and heartbreak at sea tug at our heart strings. Some people are interested in long-lost treasure, jewelry, and weapons. Others want to learn about what life was like for the people aboard the ships.

Scientists often study shipwrecks to search for clues about what happened and why. The information these scientists uncover can lead to new ideas about building and sailing ships. The lessons learned from these disasters make today's ships better and safer than ever.

Titanic resting at the bottom of the ocean

hull—the outer shell or body of a ship
artifact—an object made or used by people in the past

5

Chapter 1

THE SINKING OF THE *TITANIC*

The new ocean liner floated above the pier like a giant, floating hotel. It could carry 3,500 people, including the crew. Nearly 900-feet (274-m) long, *Titanic* was the largest ship of its time. Many people believed it was the safest ship too.

On April 10, 1912, *Titanic* left Southampton, England, for New York City. This was the ship's first voyage. More than 2,200 people were on board. They included rich and famous people, as well as poorer passengers.

The first days went smoothly. On April 14, *Titanic* received telegraph reports from other ships warning of icebergs in the area. Yet *Titanic* did not slow down as night fell.

Heading for Disaster

Two sailors watched for icebergs from the ship's crow's nest. Shortly before midnight, they spotted something. One man phoned down to the bridge. "Iceberg right ahead!" he warned.

The officer at the bridge turned hard. But it was too late. *Titanic* grazed the iceberg. The hard ice scraped along the ship's right side.

Captain Edward J. Smith had gone to his cabin for the night. He rushed to the bridge when he felt the collision. Smith went to check for damage with the ship's builder, Thomas Andrews. What they saw shocked them. Water was pouring through the hull. The ship would sink in less than two hours.

CROW'S NEST

9 DECK LEVELS

900 FEET (274 M)

crow's nest—the lookout tower of a ship
bridge—the navigation area and control center of a ship

End of *Titanic*

Titanic's passengers had two hopes for survival. Their best chance was being rescued by another ship. Captain Smith told his telegraph operator to signal other ships for help. The *Californian* was only 10 miles (16 kilometers) away. But that ship's telegraph had been turned off for the night. A *Titanic* officer also shot up signal flares. The *Californian*'s captain thought they were fireworks.

The passengers' only other hope was boarding lifeboats. But the lifeboats did not have enough room for everyone aboard. Even worse, many were not full when they were lowered into the water. *Titanic*'s 20 lifeboats had room for 1,178 people. But only about 705 were in these boats.

About an hour after the sinking, men in one of the lifeboats rowed back to the site. They were able to rescue six people from the icy waters. The rest had already died of hypothermia.

With more than 1,500 people still on board, the front of *Titanic* sank lower and lower. At 2:10 a.m., the ship tilted forward suddenly. About 10 minutes later, *Titanic* broke apart. The back end of the ship, called the stern, rose straight up before sinking into the Atlantic Ocean.

About two hours later, the *Carpathia* arrived on the scene. Its crew was only able to rescue people in the lifeboats. It had been too far away to reach *Titanic* before it sank to the bottom of the ocean.

Titanic survivors aboard the *Carpathia*

hypothermia—a life-threatening medical condition resulting from a drop in body temperature

Why and How the *Titanic* Sank

People had many questions about the *Titanic's* sinking. At first people thought the iceberg tore a big hole in the ship. But in 1996, experts examined the hull using high-tech equipment. They only found fairly small tears where the ship struck the iceberg.

Some researchers now think parts of the ship were built with low-quality metal. Tests were performed on parts of *Titanic* raised from the ocean floor. Some of the pins that held the ship together, called rivets, were made of poor iron. The collision may have popped them out.

—— tears from where the iceberg hit

1. *Titanic's* hull had 16 sections. The ship could float if four sections flooded. But the iceberg opened holes in five sections. Water flooded into and weighed down the front of the ship.

MISTAKES MADE

What led to the *Titanic* disaster? Experts agree on several factors. First, the captain should have posted more crewmen to watch for icebergs. Second, those crewmen should have had binoculars. Third, the ship should have slowed down. *Titanic*'s high speed made it impossible to avoid the iceberg.

Other problems occurred after the collision. The crew and passengers had not practiced lifeboat drills. Not everyone knew where to go or what to do during the emergency. More importantly, there was a shortage of lifeboats. *Titanic* had more lifeboats than rules required at that time. But there were not nearly enough for everyone on board.

2. The front of the ship sank, raising the back end out of the water.

3. The stress broke the hull apart, and the ship quickly sank.

Chapter 2

WHY SHIPS SINK

Every shipwreck contains a mystery. The evidence scientists need to solve that mystery is often far beneath the surface of the ocean. After a sinking, people want to learn what sent the ship to the sea floor. Knowing why may help sailors avoid future disasters.

FACT: In 1820 a whale rammed the whaling ship *Essex*. The ship sank. The wreck became the idea for the book *Moby Dick*.

There are two main reasons why ships go down—nature and human error. Ships sink because of rough seas caused by bad weather. Human mistakes may include bad navigation, overlooked repairs, or a poorly trained crew. Shipwrecks are often the result of both nature's power and people's mistakes.

ICEBREAKER

Hitting Ice

In cold, deep seas, icebergs can punch holes in ships. Ships called icebreakers have extra-thick hulls to break up ice and clear a path for other ships. Icebreakers must travel at slow speeds. Their captains must watch for ice that is too thick to break up.

Running Aground

Bad weather or poor piloting often sends a vessel hitting land or crashing into rocks. In March 1989, the *Exxon Valdez* oil tanker was sailing along the coast of Alaska. An officer mistakenly steered the tanker into shallow water. It hit the rocks, causing a huge oil spill.

Stormy Weather

Piloting a ship looks easy on a calm day, but stormy weather is a different story. Strong winds and big waves can beat up a ship and even tear it apart.

In September 1980, the MV *Derbyshire* was approaching Japan. The huge bulk carrier was loaded with iron ore. It was caught in a terrible typhoon. The high winds and big waves hammered the ship. Amid the storm, the ship seemed to disappear. The 44 people on board didn't even have time to send a distress call.

FACT: In 1995, the cruise liner *Queen Elizabeth 2* survived a huge 90-foot (27-m) wave.

Searchers found the wreck in 1994. They sent down a remotely operated vehicle (ROV) to take pictures. It found that the *Derbyshire's* front hatch covers had caved in. Hatch covers are like doors that lie flat on the deck. They open up to the ship's interior. Big waves or a **rogue wave** were the likely cause. Water from the waves most likely caved in the hatch covers, quickly sinking the ship.

Rogue Waves

Imagine an ocean wave as tall as a 10-story building coming out of nowhere. Now picture it heading for your ship. These rogue waves are also called monster waves or freak waves. They are much bigger than normal waves and can flip or smash a ship. Rogue waves can reach 200 feet (61 m) high.

Experts used to think rogue waves were just myths because no one had ever measured one. But in 1995 a rogue wave hit an oil platform. The wave measured 84 feet (26 m) high. Now scientists think rogue waves may be more common than they once believed.

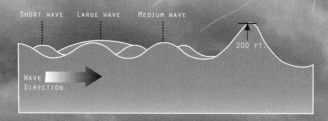

SHORT WAVE   LARGE WAVE   MEDIUM WAVE

200 FT.

WAVE DIRECTION

Experts think these waves have two main causes. The first is when smaller waves randomly join together. They may combine to form a giant wave.

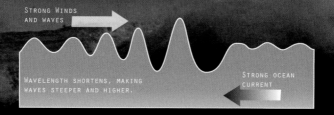

STRONG WINDS AND WAVES

WAVELENGTH SHORTENS, MAKING WAVES STEEPER AND HIGHER.

STRONG OCEAN CURRENT

The second cause is when wind pushes waves against strong ocean currents. Fighting against the natural flow of the water causes waves to build up in size and power.

typhoon—a powerful storm in the Pacific Ocean; typhoons are called hurricanes or tropical cyclones in other parts of the world
rogue wave—a huge, breaking wall of water that seems to come out of nowhere; rogue waves are rare but evidence supports their existence

Ship-to-Ship Accidents

Ship-to-ship collisions can result in terrible wrecks. These accidents are often the result of carelessness.

On the night of December 20, 1987, the ferry *Doña Paz* was transporting passengers in the Philippines. The *Vector,* a tanker, was loaded down with oil and gasoline. The two ships collided. Oil from the *Vector* spilled into the ocean. Both ships and the water around them erupted in flames. The ships sank quickly. More than 4,000 people died. Only 24 people on the *Doña Paz* survived. Just two people on the *Vector* were as lucky.

The crash was the result of poor navigation by the *Doña Paz* crew. A survivor reported that only an officer in training was on the bridge.

Philippines

Limay

Tacloban City

RED course of the *Vector*
PURPLE course of the *Doña Paz*
X collision

Some survivors from the *Doña Paz* reported that the ship's crew had been having a Christmas party. Witnesses claimed the captain was at the party.

Wartime Targets

During wartime enemy ships attack each other. Aircraft may blast enemy ships with bombs. Submarines may sink them with torpedoes. Ships may also strike mines. These underwater bombs explode when a ship hits them.

The *Britannic* was built to be a passenger liner. It was turned into a hospital ship during World War I (1914–1918). In 1916 the *Britannic* struck a mine near Greece while going to pick up wounded soldiers. It sank in 55 minutes. The crew got most people into lifeboats. More than 1,000 people were on board, but only 30 died.

WILLIAM GARZKE, SHIPWRECK INVESTIGATOR

William Garzke works with the Society of Naval Architects and Marine Engineers. Like a crime scene investigator, he studies shipwrecks in search of clues about why they sank. He has investigated dozens of shipwrecks in his long career. Garzke looks for five things to help him investigate a wreck:

1. wind, wave, and weather conditions when the ship sank
2. the most recent design drawings of the ship
3. the ship's log and recordings of any radio calls
4. statements from survivors about what happened
5. underwater photos of the wreck site

Deadly Mistakes

Everyone makes mistakes. But even a small error on a big ship can mean disaster. In 1987 such a mistake **capsized** the *Herald of Free Enterprise*. This ship was a car ferry. It carried people and cars between England and other European ports.

Cars drove into the ship through giant doors in the back end. The doors were supposed to be shut for the trip. But on one trip in 1987, a crewman forgot to close them.

When the ship sailed, water flooded through the open doors. With the slightest tilt of the ship, all the water sloshed heavily to one side. Experts call this the free surface effect. The ship tipped and suddenly rolled over.

There was no time to launch lifeboats. Luckily, the ferry flipped onto a sandbank and did not sink. If the ship had sunk, passengers would have been stuck in the boat as it filled with water. Four hundred people survived the terrifying accident, but 193 people did not.

FLIP A SHIP: THE FREE SURFACE EFFECT

The free surface effect can flip a ship. Picture a ferry that has taken on water. When the ship rocks to one side, the water moves that direction. What happens when the ship rocks back the other way? The water pauses. Then it slams over to the other side. This action builds momentum. This sloshing gets stronger as the ship rocks, eventually causing it to roll over.

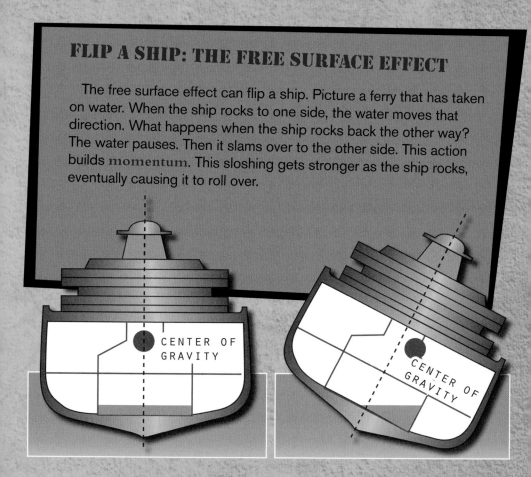

CENTER OF GRAVITY

CENTER OF GRAVITY

capsize—to tip over in water
momentum—the force or speed created by movement

Ship Failure

Ships are big machines with thousands of working parts. A ship's crew must make sure a ship is in good working order.

In December 2004, the *Selendang Ayu* left Seattle, Washington, with 26 crew members on board. The ship was hauling a load of soybeans to China. Before long the *Selendang Ayu*'s engines began having problems. The captain shut down the engines to make repairs. But high winds and big waves pushed the ship toward the Alaskan coast. The crew could not restart the engines. Other ships tried to tow the *Selendang Ayu* to deeper water, but the seas were too rough. The ship was headed for disaster.

Coast Guard helicopters flew in to rescue the crew. They were able to save 20 men. Unfortunately, one of the helicopters crashed, killing six people. The ship eventually hit the rocks and ripped in two, spilling oil along the coast.

Coast Guard rescuing the crew of the *Selendang Ayu*

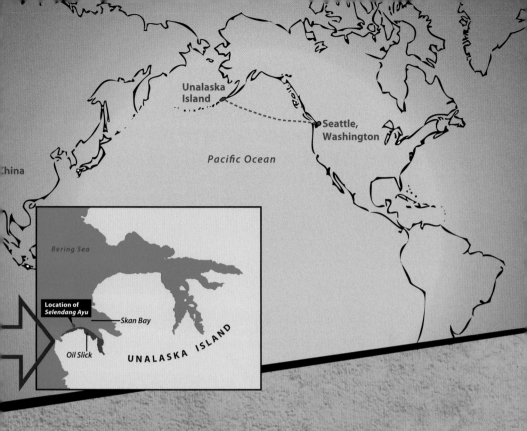

Unalaska
Island

Seattle,
Washington

Pacific Ocean

China

Bering Sea

Location of
Selendang Ayu

Skan Bay

Oil Slick

UNALASKA ISLAND

Fire

A fire at sea can be disastrous. Flames spread quickly,
and smoke can kill people trapped aboard a ship.

In November 1965, the *Yarmouth Castle* left Miami,
Florida, on a Caribbean cruise. A fire started in a
storage room and soon was burning out of control.
It scorched the deck and other wooden parts of the
ship. The fire fed off new paint on the walls.

The crew was not ready for such an emergency. The
ship's fire hoses didn't have enough water pressure to
fight the fire. The ship's sprinkler system also failed to
activate. Some of the lifeboats were stuck to the ship by
layers of new paint. The captain and members of the crew
fled the ship without helping the passengers. Luckily,
nearby ships came to the rescue. Hundreds of people
were saved, but 90 people died.

Chapter 3

BUILDING A SAFER SHIP

For as long as ships have sailed, shipbuilders have been trying to increase ship safety. Certain features help meet this goal.

The basic structure of a ship must be strong to withstand the forces of nature at sea. Good buoyancy helps a ship float high in the water.

A strong hull: The hull takes a pounding from powerful waves. It should be made of strong metal. Tankers and some cruise ships have double hulls that give an extra layer of safety. If the outer hull gets damaged, the inner hull will keep the ship afloat.

Fireproofing: Though ships are surrounded by water, fire remains a serious threat. Today's vessels are built with as many fireproof materials as possible. Smoke alarms are placed throughout the ships. Engine rooms must have systems for quickly putting out fires.

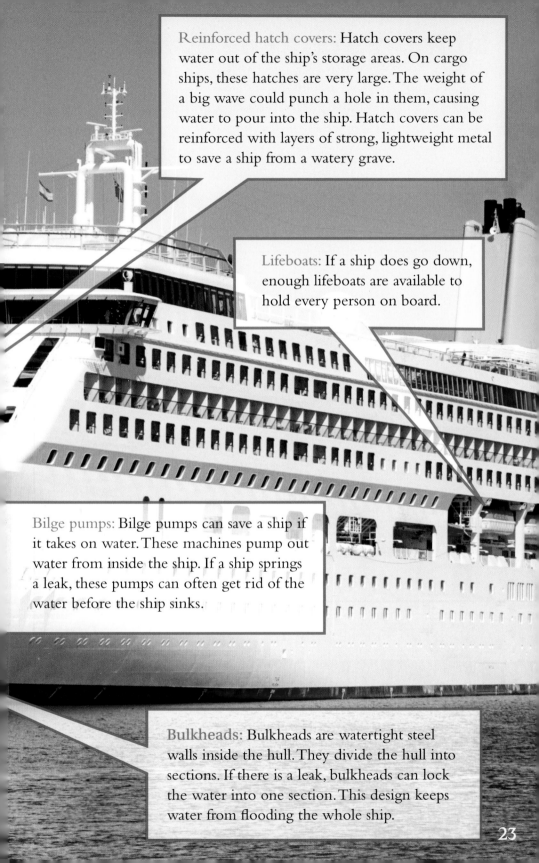

Reinforced hatch covers: Hatch covers keep water out of the ship's storage areas. On cargo ships, these hatches are very large. The weight of a big wave could punch a hole in them, causing water to pour into the ship. Hatch covers can be reinforced with layers of strong, lightweight metal to save a ship from a watery grave.

Lifeboats: If a ship does go down, enough lifeboats are available to hold every person on board.

Bilge pumps: Bilge pumps can save a ship if it takes on water. These machines pump out water from inside the ship. If a ship springs a leak, these pumps can often get rid of the water before the ship sinks.

Bulkheads: Bulkheads are watertight steel walls inside the hull. They divide the hull into sections. If there is a leak, bulkheads can lock the water into one section. This design keeps water from flooding the whole ship.

Lifeboats and Life Rafts

Ships carry lifeboats and life rafts to save passengers if a ship runs into trouble. Lifeboats have a hard hull. Life rafts inflate so they will float. Both have covers to protect people from sun and rain. Some lifeboats or life rafts can hold up to 100 people.

FACT

The International Maritime Organization makes safety rules about shipbuilding, crew training, and life-saving equipment on ships.

Some life rafts are stored in chests. These chests can be tossed overboard in an emergency. With a yank on a rope, the raft inflates. Other life rafts will actually inflate on their own as a ship sinks.

According to current rules, all ships must have enough lifeboats or life rafts to carry everyone on board. They must also have enough life jackets for all passengers and crew.

In an emergency, people must be able to get off the ship quickly. Cruise liners now have slides to help passengers escape. People scoot down these slides to reach a life raft.

Most lifeboats hang on the side of the ship. From there, they can be quickly lowered to the water.

Some very large ships use "free-fall lifeboats." These lifeboats are set on ramps. This design allows people to quickly slide off a sinking ship instead of having to jump in the water.

Crew Training and Drills

As leaders of a ship's crew, officers must be ready for anything. Their jobs require the courage to do the right thing. They must not take needless risks.

Good training turns a crew into a strong team. They must know how to work the lifeboats and what to do if a fire breaks out. They should know how to get people off the ship quickly and safely. Being well-prepared prevents people from panicking.

People must act quickly in emergencies. There may not be time to think about what to do. That is why all cruise ships hold lifeboat drills for passengers. Passengers and crew members must know where to go and what to do if the ship is in danger of sinking.

Ship Simulators

How does a sailor learn to pilot a ferry? Where can a captain practice docking a huge cruise ship? Officers can now practice on ship simulators. Training simulators look just like the real bridge of a ship.

Simulators let people make mistakes on a computer. Practicing there is a lot less dangerous than practicing at sea. The computer lets sailors test their skills in different situations. It can cook up a big storm or pretend something is wrong with the engines. Some simulators are even built on platforms. They can shake and roll like a real ship in rough seas.

SURVIVAL KITS

After a shipwreck, people may be stuck on a lifeboat for hours or days. They must be able to survive until rescuers reach them. That is why lifeboats and life rafts contain survival kits. Survival kits usually include:

- food and water
- flashlights
- flares
- fishing kit
- first-aid kit and medicine

- patch kit to fix the raft
- radio to call for help
- emergency beacons to guide rescuers

Chapter 4

ON THE BRIDGE

For a ship's crew, knowledge is safety. The more the officers know, the easier it is for them to make good decisions. Some high-tech tools help today's sailors navigate safely.

The bridges of today's ships are loaded with computers and electronics. From this command center, officers can tell how the ship is running. They can check weather reports, charts, the ship's exact position and course, and possible obstacles ahead.

Radar

Radar helps protect ships from colliding with icebergs, rocks, and other ships. Radar shoots out radio waves that travel in all directions. When the waves hit something solid, they bounce back. The radar receiver figures out how far away objects are. It creates a map that helps the crew navigate.

SENDER/RECEIVER

OBJECT

ORIGINAL WAVE

Navigation and GPS

Navigation charts show coastlines, lighthouses, rocks, and water depth. Today's ships have electronic charts that are used with a Global Positioning System (GPS).

Crew members use GPS to figure out the ship's course. The GPS relies on **satellites** in space. Twenty-four GPS satellites orbit Earth. Each satellite continually beams down a signal. The GPS unit on a ship searches for the signals. It seeks out signals from at least four satellites and uses them to calculate the ship's position.

Chartplotter

A chartplotter takes the ship's location from the GPS unit and figures out the ship's speed and direction. Its digital display shows a map of the area around the ship. It may even tell the crew how to steer to its destination.

satellite—a device that circles Earth; satellites take pictures or send and receive signals to and from Earth

WEATHER INSTRUMENTS. Ship crews get weather reports online or by radio. These reports predict wave height and the speed and direction of the wind over large areas. Forecasts alert ship crews of nearby storms. Some computer programs suggest different routes to avoid bad weather.

CHARTPLOTTER

RADAR

The emergency radio channel for ships is Channel 16. Crew members on big ships and people at rescue stations listen to this channel 24 hours a day.

DEPTH FINDER. Depth finders send sound waves into the water. The waves bounce off the sea floor and back to the ship. Then the device calculates the water's depth.

ONBOARD RADIOS. Radios let ships contact each other and allow crews to quickly call for help in an emergency.

WARNING SENSORS AND ALARMS. Crews are alerted if there is a problem anywhere on the ship.

RESCUE AT SEA

"Mayday, mayday, mayday!" Captain Eric Peter Jacobsen radioed for help. It was 2:30 a.m. on March 23, 2008. Jacobsen's fishing vessel, the *Alaska Ranger*, was sinking. Water flooded the back of the ship. No one knew how to stop it.

Alaska Ranger had 47 crew members. All of them had pulled on survival suits to keep their bodies warm in cold water. The ship was sinking in the Bering Sea, one of the world's coldest, stormiest seas.

ALASKA RANGER

SEATTLE

Alaska Ranger tipped far to the right. "Abandon ship!" the captain ordered. Only 22 people were able to get into the life rafts. The rest jumped overboard. The lights on their suits bobbed in the dark water. They watched their ship disappear beneath the waves.

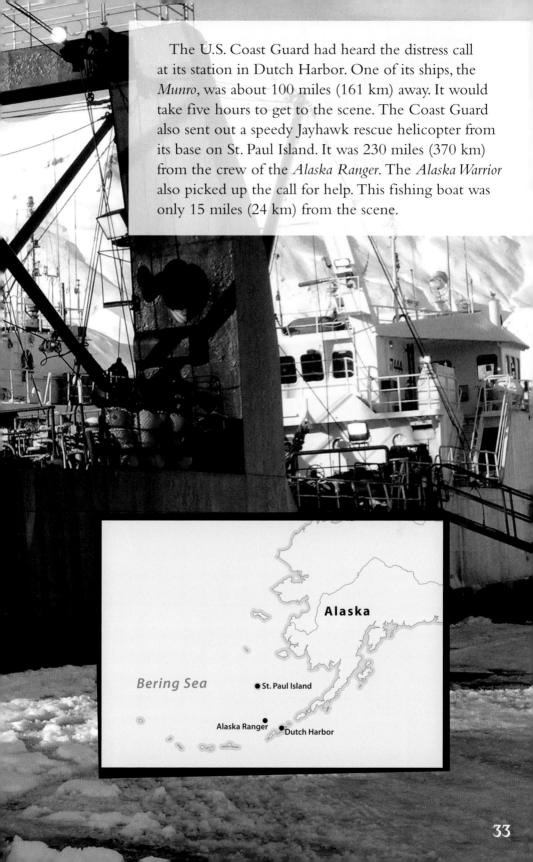

The U.S. Coast Guard had heard the distress call at its station in Dutch Harbor. One of its ships, the *Munro*, was about 100 miles (161 km) away. It would take five hours to get to the scene. The Coast Guard also sent out a speedy Jayhawk rescue helicopter from its base on St. Paul Island. It was 230 miles (370 km) from the crew of the *Alaska Ranger*. The *Alaska Warrior* also picked up the call for help. This fishing boat was only 15 miles (24 km) from the scene.

Alaska

Bering Sea

● St. Paul Island

Alaska Ranger ●
● Dutch Harbor

SURVIVING IN COLD WATER

Cold water quickly saps a person's strength. Just a few minutes in water that is 32 degrees Fahrenheit (0 degrees Celsius) makes arms and legs useless. After a while, hypothermia sets in.

If the water temperature is …	A person will die in …
Less than 32°F (0°C)	45 minutes or less
32.5–40°F (0–5°C)	30 to 90 minutes
40–50°F (5–10°C)	1 to 3 hours
50–60°F (10–15°C)	1 to 6 hours
60–70°F (15–21°C)	2 to 40 hours

2. The Jayhawk helicopter got to the scene around 5 a.m. The crew spotted the men's lights in the sea below.

1. The men in the bitterly cold water were running out of time. The survival suits helped, but their bodies were growing weaker.

JAYHAWK
HELICOPTER

25 PEOPLE IN
THE WATER

22 PEOPLE IN
2 LIFE RAFTS

1 OVERTURNED
LIFE RAFT

While the Coast Guard pulled survivors out of the water, the *Alaska Warrior* rescued the people in life rafts.

6. By 6 a.m. the *Munro* was still about 75 miles (121 km) away. But it was close enough to launch its own Dolphin helicopter. This helicopter was smaller than the Jayhawk and could not fly as far. But it was able to lift five more men from the cold water.

3. The hovering helicopter lowered a rescue basket and a rescue diver. The diver helped each man get into the basket. One by one, they were pulled from the sea.

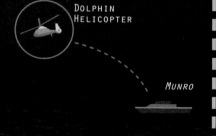

DOLPHIN
HELICOPTER

MUNRO

5. The helicopter had to fly to the *Munro*.

ALASKA
WARRIOR

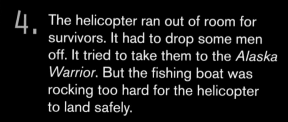

4. The helicopter ran out of room for survivors. It had to drop some men off. It tried to take them to the *Alaska Warrior*. But the fishing boat was rocking too hard for the helicopter to land safely.

After the Disaster

One crewman from the *Alaska Ranger* was never found. The searchers recovered the bodies of four others. One of the dead was Captain Jacobsen. The rescuers saved the 42 others. The helicopter crews all received medals for bravery.

The question remained of why the big fishing boat sank. Investigators think the vessel's rudder probably broke off. This would have caused the stern to flood quickly. They also concluded that the ship had other safety problems and that the crew was not properly trained.

Coast Guard rescuers help *an Alaska Ranger* survivor onto the *Munro.*

No one will ever know exactly what happened to the *Alaska Ranger*. The boat now rests 6,000 feet (1,829 m) beneath the surface of the Bering Sea.

LIFE VESTS AND "GUMBY SUITS"

Early life vests were filled with cork. Most life vests today are made with foam, and some can be inflated. They are brightly colored and may have whistles and lights attached. These features help rescuers find survivors.

But life vests cannot protect people from cold water. That is why many ships carry survival suits nicknamed "Gumby suits." They are shaped like the clay cartoon character "Gumby." The suits are made of thick foam and cover everything but the face. These suits keep people warm and afloat in cold water.

"Mayday, mayday, mayday" is how sailors radio for help. The term comes from *m'aidez*, the French word for "help me." It is said three times to prevent confusion.

Chapter 6

FAMOUS SHIPWRECKS

Lusitania (1915)

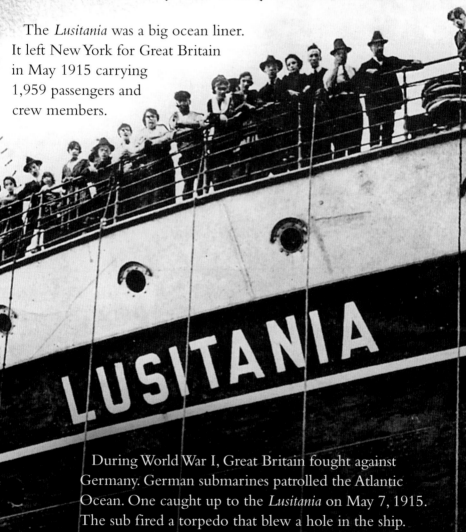

The *Lusitania* was a big ocean liner. It left New York for Great Britain in May 1915 carrying 1,959 passengers and crew members.

During World War I, Great Britain fought against Germany. German submarines patrolled the Atlantic Ocean. One caught up to the *Lusitania* on May 7, 1915. The sub fired a torpedo that blew a hole in the ship. Another explosion erupted inside the ship. The *Lusitania* sank in just 18 minutes. About 1,200 people died.

The *Lusitania* was a passenger ship, but German leaders claimed it was also carrying war supplies. The British and U.S. governments denied this claim.

Wilhelm Gustloff (1945)

During World War II (1939–1945), thousands of ships were sunk. But one ship went down with the largest loss of life in recorded history. The *Wilhelm Gustloff* was a huge passenger ship carrying mostly women and children escaping the fighting in Germany.

A Soviet submarine spotted the ship. It tracked the *Wilhelm Gustloff* and launched three torpedoes. The ship sank in just 45 minutes. More than 9,000 people died.

World War II sub torpedo

DIVING FOR CLUES

In September 1994, the *Estonia*, a passenger ferry, sank in the Baltic Sea. More than 800 people died. In November 1994, investigators sent scuba divers to look for clues about what happened.

The divers dropped 250 feet (76 m) into the dark water to explore the wreck. Diving in deep water causes dangerous gases to build up in the body. The divers used a special mix of oxygen and other gases in their tanks to help reduce the risk.

The dive teams inspected the front end of the *Estonia* very carefully. They had to avoid sharp objects that could slice their scuba gear and leave them helpless deep underwater.

Upon inspection, the divers found that a door on the front end had not been locked correctly. Strong waves had torn the door from its hinges. The ship then took on water and sank.

Andrea Doria (1956)

The *Andrea Doria* was an Italian ocean liner sailing to New York City with about 1,700 people on board. The ship was caught in thick fog on the evening of July 25, 1956. Its radar spotted a ship approaching. It was the *Stockholm*, a smaller passenger ship. The officers on both ships thought the other was turning a different way. The two ships accidentally steered into each other's path. The officers tried to stop at the last second, but it was too late.

Andrea Doria sinking

The *Stockholm* rammed into the side of the Andrea *Doria*. Water poured into the *Andrea Doria*, and the ship tilted. The tilting made it impossible to lower lifeboats. Both ships radioed for help, and nearby vessels soon showed up. They launched their lifeboats to help rescue passengers. By the next morning, all of the survivors were safe. But 46 people had died in the collision.

FACT: Robert Hudson was the last survivor off the *Andrea Doria*. He had slept through the collision and awoke in the morning to an empty, tilted ship.

The front end of the *Stockholm* was crushed, but the ship did not sink. *Andrea Doria* was not so lucky. It sank about 11 hours after the collision.

Stockholm after impact

MIRACLE GIRL OF THE ANDREA DORIA

Fourteen-year-old Linda Morgan was asleep in her cabin on the *Andrea Doria*. Her younger half sister was in the other bunk. They were scheduled to dock in New York the next morning.

Linda was jolted awake when the *Andrea Doria* and *Stockholm* collided. She looked around and did not know where she was. Amazingly, Linda was on the deck of the *Stockholm*. The impact had thrown her onto the other ship. People called her "the miracle girl" of the *Andrea Doria*. Sadly, Linda's half sister and stepfather were killed in the collision.

Edmund Fitzgerald (1975)

The *Edmund Fitzgerald* was a big **freighter**. It carried cargo on the Great Lakes. In November 1975, the ship was crossing Lake Superior. It was hauling a heavy load to a steel mill. The *Edmund Fitzgerald* sailed into a terrible winter storm. Powerful winds and big waves soon knocked out the ship's radar. A nearby ship, the *Arthur M. Anderson*, helped the *Edmund Fitzgerald* navigate over the radio. The captains of the ships agreed to sail to safety at a nearby port.

The *Edmund Fitzgerald* never made it. The captain had reported that the ship was taking on water. Waves were washing over the deck. Suddenly, the *Edmund Fitzgerald* disappeared from the *Arthur M. Anderson*'s radar. It had sunk straight to the bottom of the lake.

FACT

The *Edmund Fitzgerald* was only 17 miles (27 km) from a safe harbor when it sank.

42

Gordon Lightfoot's hit song, "The Wreck of the *Edmund Fitzgerald*" honors the doomed ship and its crew.

EDMUND FITZGERALD

The cause of the *Edmund Fitzgerald*'s sinking remains a mystery. The Coast Guard thought big waves might have caved in the deck hatches, and water poured into the ship. Another possibility is that a rogue wave sank the freighter.

freighter—a ship that carries cargo

Le Joola (2002)

Le Joola was a passenger ferry that carried people back and forth along the west coast of Africa. It was built to carry about 600 people. But on September 26, 2002, there were nearly 2,000 people on board. That night *Le Joola* sailed into a storm. Experts think the overcrowded ship was too heavy to withstand the large waves. Amid the storm, the ship suddenly flipped over. Many people were trapped inside. Fishermen came out to the wreck to help. They rescued some passengers, but 1,863 people drowned.

Passengers boarding *Le Joola*

Explorer (2007)

The *Explorer* was a small cruise ship that carried tourists to Antarctica. It had an extra-thick hull to bash through ice.

Explorer sinking

In 2007, the ship went into a field of icebergs near Antarctica. It sprang a leak, and water began to pour in. The ship was soon tilting to the right. The captain radioed for help and loaded the lifeboats. Three ships arrived within hours. All 100 tourists and 54 crew members of the *Explorer* were safe. The ship sank about 20 hours after the accident.

Ships face risks every time they go to sea. Whether it's an unsafe ship, a foolish mistake, or just plain bad luck, every shipwreck has its causes. Learning from such disasters helps create a safer future on the high seas.

GLOSSARY

artifact (AR-tuh-fakt)—an object made or used by people in the past

bridge (BRIJ)—the control center of a ship

capsize (KAP-syz)—to tip over in the water

crow's nest (KROHS NEST)—a small platform used for a lookout, found on top of a sailing ship

ferry (FAYR-ee)—a boat or ship that regularly carries people across a stretch of water

frieghter (FRAY-tur)—a ship that carries cargo

hull (HULL)—the outer shell or body of a ship

hypothermia (hye-puh-THUR-mee-uh)—a life-threatening medical condition resulting from a drop in body temperature

momentum (moh-MEN-tuhm)—the force or speed created by movement

navigation (nav-uh-GAY-shun)—using instruments and charts to find your way in a ship or other vehicle

rogue wave (ROHG WAYV)—huge, breaking walls of water that seem to come out of nowhere; rogue waves are rare but evidence supports their existence

satellite (SAT-uh-lite)—a device that circles Earth; satellites take pictures or send signals to Earth and receive signals from Earth

typhoon (tye-FOON)—a powerful storm with high winds and large waves that happens in the Pacific Ocean; typhoons are called hurricanes and tropical cyclones in other parts of the world

READ MORE

Cerullo, Mary M. *Shipwrecks: Exploring Sunken Cities Beneath the Sea.* New York: Dutton Children's Books, 2009.

Griffith, Anita. *The 10 Most Unforgettable Shipwrecks.* New York: Children's Press, 2007.

MacDonald, Fiona. *100 Things You Should Know About Ship-wrecks.* 100 Things You Should Know. Broomall, Pa.: Mason Crest Publishers, 2009.

O'Shei, Tim. *How to Survive Being Lost at Sea.* Prepare to Survive. Mankato, Minn.: Capstone Press, 2009.

Pipe, Jim. *Titanic.* Richmond Hill, Ontario, Canada: Firefly Books, 2007.

INTERNET SITES

FactHound offers a safe, fun way to find Internet sites related to this book. All of the sites on FactHound have been researched by our staff.

Here's all you do:

Visit *www.facthound.com*

Type in this code: 9781429647946

INDEX

Alaska Ranger, 32–37
Alaska Warrior, 33, 34, 35
Andrea Doria, 40–41
Arthur M. Anderson, 42

bad weather, 13, 14, 27, 30, 42, 44
Britannic, 17
building ships, 5, 10, 22–23, 24

Californian, 8
Carpathia, 9
chartplotters, 29, 30
Coast Guard, 20, 33, 34–35, 43
crew training, 13, 24, 26, 36

depth finders, 31
Doña Paz, 16

Edmund Fitzgerald, 42–43
Essex, 12
Estonia, 39
Explorer, 45
Exxon Valdez, 13

fires, 21, 22, 26
free surface effect, 18–19

Garzke, William, 17
Global Positioning Systems
   (GPS), 29

Herald of Free Enterprise, 18
hypothermia, 9, 34

icebergs, 6–7, 10, 11, 13, 29
icebreakers, 13, 45
International Maritime
   Organization, 24
investigating shipwrecks, 10, 12,
   14, 17, 36, 39

Le Joola, 44
lifeboats, 8, 9, 11, 17, 19, 21,
   23, 24–25, 26, 27, 40, 45

life rafts, 24–25, 27, 32
Lusitania, 38

Munro, 33, 35
MV *Derbyshire*, 14

navigation, 13, 16, 28, 29, 42
navigation charts, 29

oil spills, 13, 16, 20

parts of a ship
   bilge pumps, 23
   bridges, 6, 7, 27, 28–31
   bulkheads, 23
   crow's nests, 6
   engines, 20, 27
   hatch covers, 14, 23, 43
   hulls, 4, 7, 10, 11, 13, 22, 23,
      24, 45
   rudders, 36
   sterns, 9, 36

Queen Elizabeth 2, 14

radar, 29, 30, 40, 42
radios, 30, 31, 32, 37, 40, 42, 45
rogue waves, 14–15, 43

Selendang Ayu, 20
ship simulators, 27
ship-to-ship accidents, 16, 29,
   40–41
Stockholm, 40–41
survival kits, 27
survival suits, 32, 34, 37

telegraph, 6, 8
Titanic, 4, 6–11

Vector, 16

wartime targets, 17, 38, 39
Wilhelm Gustloff, 39

Yarmouth Castle, 21